TUDOR 1485–1603	STUART 1603–1714	GEORGIAN 1714–1837	VICTORIAN 1837–1901	MODERN TIMES 1901–NOW

Children's HISTORY of DEVON

Written by
Tina Orr Munro

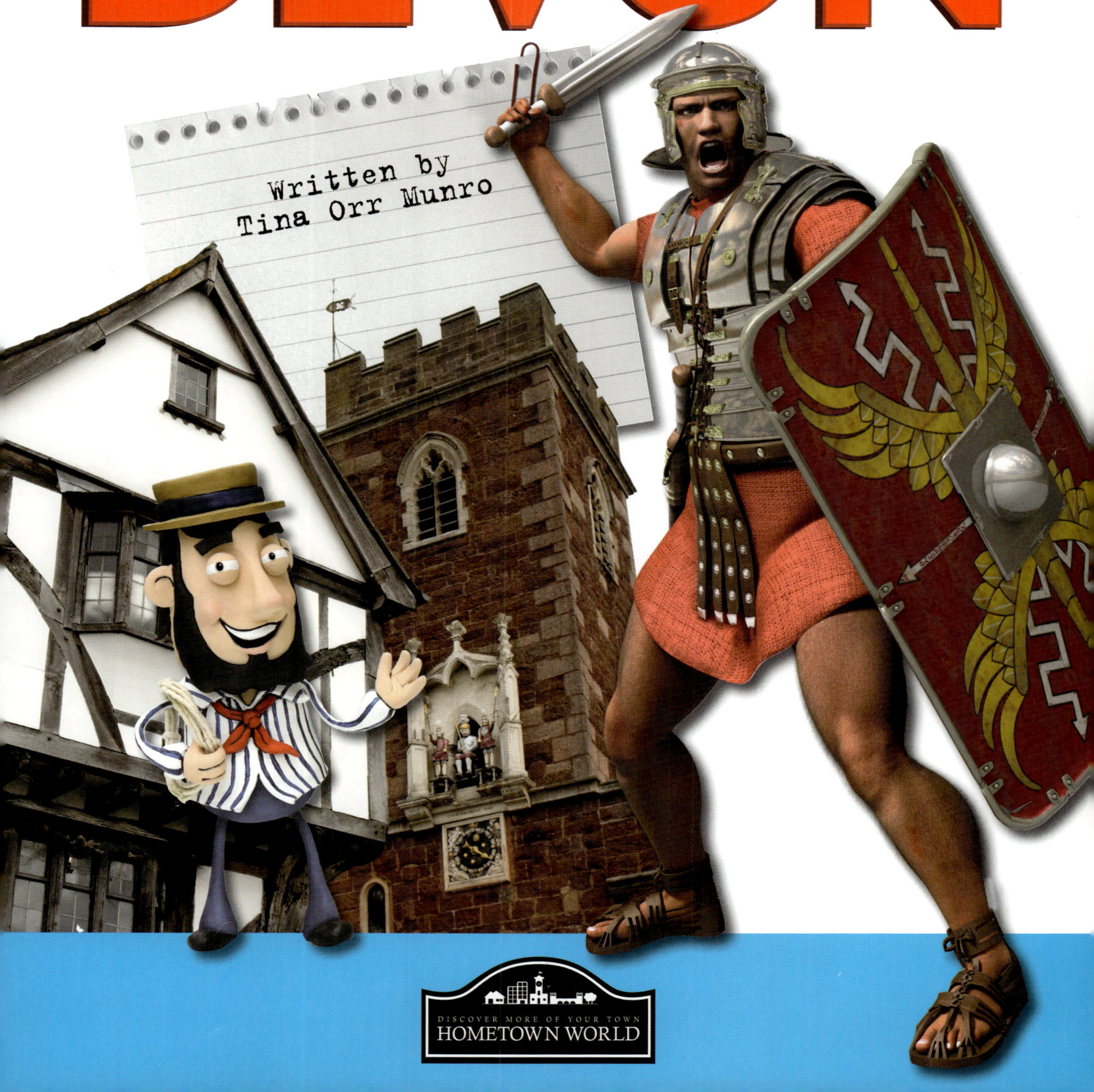

DISCOVER MORE OF YOUR TOWN
HOMETOWN WORLD

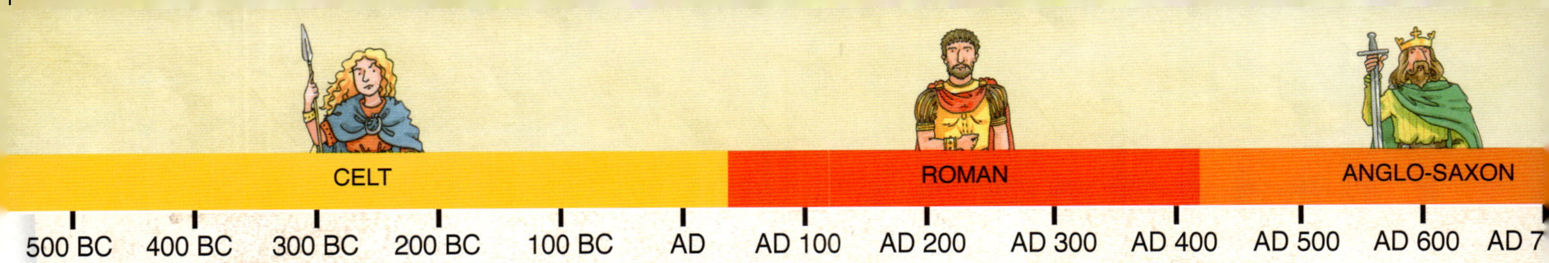

How well do you know Devon?

Have you ever wondered what it would have been like living in Devon when the Romans arrived? What about when the first ever railways were built? This book will uncover the important and exciting things that happened in this wonderful county.

Want to hear the other good bits? Some rather brainy folk have worked on this book to make sure it's fun and informative. So what are you waiting for? Peel back the pages and be amazed at Devon's very own story.

Timeline shows which period (dates and people) each spread is talking about

'Spot this!' game with hints on something to find in the county

THE FACTS

Fun Facts to amaze you!

THE EVIDENCE

Intriguing photos

An imaginary account of what it was like for children growing up in Devon

A summary explaining how we know about the past

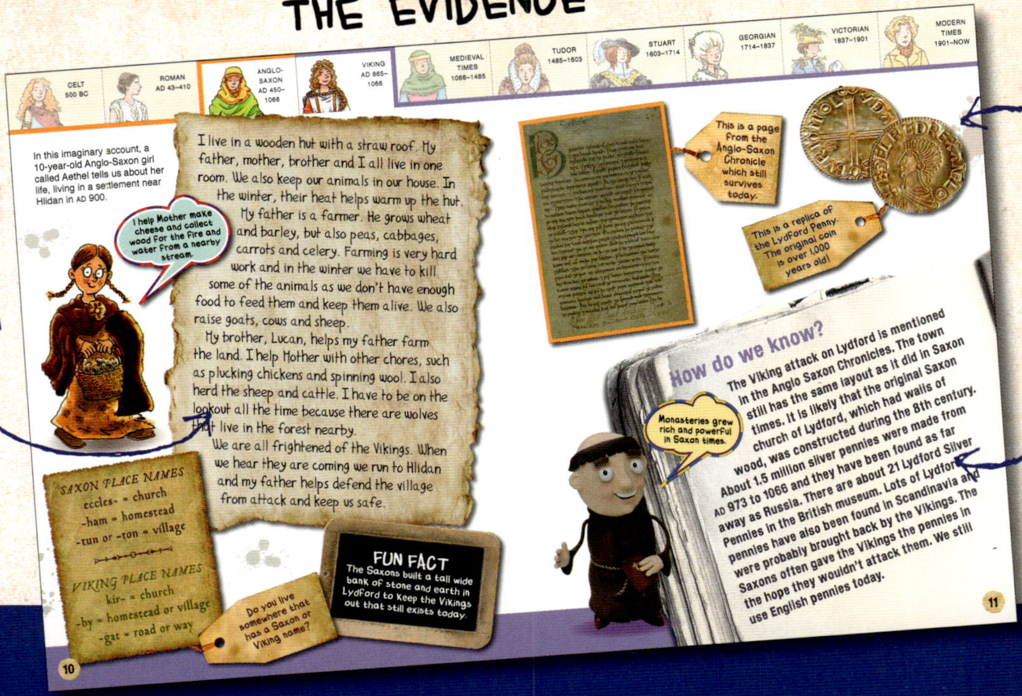

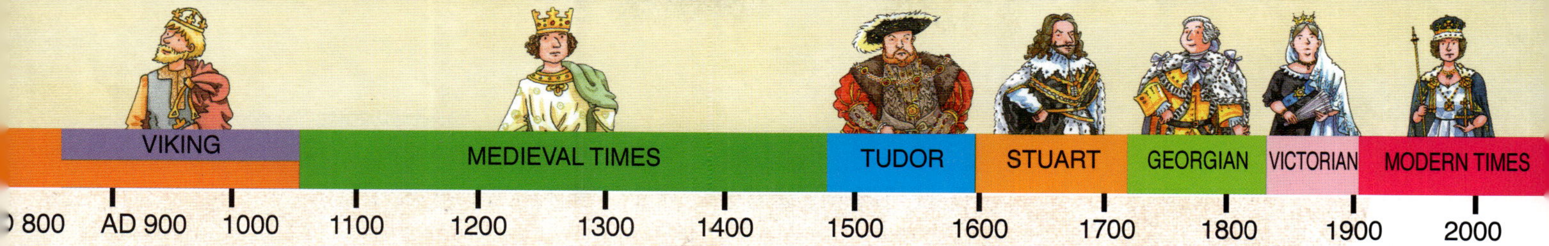
VIKING
MEDIEVAL TIMES
TUDOR
STUART
GEORGIAN
VICTORIAN
MODERN TIMES
800
AD 900
1000
1100
1200
1300
1400
1500
1600
1700
1800
1900
2000

Contents

ROMAN Defenders

Claudius marches through the fast-flowing river Exe with the other soldiers. At last the fort town of Isca comes into view. Claudius has walked for miles in the scorching sun. He is tired. His armour, which is made of iron and leather, is very heavy and his wool tunic itches his skin, but he is pleased to reach Isca unhurt. In the surrounding woods and hills, he knows tribes of Celts are waiting to attack him and the other soldiers and drive them out of their land.

This shows what the Roman settlement of Isca Dumnoniorum (Exeter) may have looked like.

Who were the Romans?

The Romans invaded Britain in AD 43. They came from Italy, and had built up a huge empire which covered most of Europe. Their next step was to cross the English Channel. Why did they come to Britain? There was a new Roman emperor, called Claudius, who wanted to show he was a bold and warlike leader. He also wanted Britain's riches, such as grain, tin, iron and gold.

The powerful Roman army landed in south-east England. Quickly, it took control of the area where London now stands. From here, smaller forces set out to the west and the north to conquer more land.

By about AD 100, the Romans ruled most of the south and west of Britain. But they never conquered the far north of England or Scotland, or took control of Wales. Nor did they try to invade Ireland.

...AD 43 ROMANS INVADE BRITAIN...AD 50 ROMANS ARRIVE IN DEVON...

Fort Isca

The Romans arrived in Devon in around AD 50. Roman soldiers built a wooden fort on a hill near the river Exe because it was the easiest place to cross the river. They called the fort Isca. Isca was the Celtic word for river or water. Today it is called Exeter.

To begin with, around 5,000 Roman soldiers defended the area from local Celtic tribes, but life was fairly peaceful and the soldiers left in AD 75. The fort was replaced by a Roman town which had a market place, shops and a basilica, which is a type of town hall. In AD 200 the Romans built a wall to protect the city from the Celts and to show the power of the Roman Empire. The wall was an amazing 2,500 metres long! Large parts of the wall remain today.

SPOT THIS!

Can you spot the red brick taken from a nearby extinct volcano and used by the Romans to build the city walls?

A typical Roman Fort

Towns and Roads

The Romans changed the landscape of Britain in many ways. They built towns and forts, as centres for governing areas they had conquered. Between these they laid a network of roads, so that soldiers could move quickly from place to place. A later Roman emperor, Hadrian, also ordered the building of a wall in the far north. Its aim was to keep Roman territory separate from the barbarians on the other side.

FUN FACT

The original city wall built by the Romans was six metres high. That's the height of one and a half double decker buses!

Once the Romans settled, they kept many of their Roman ways of life. This is an imaginary account of Aurelius, a young Roman boy living in Exeter in AD 200. He is 10 years old and lives with his mother, and his father who is a merchant.

FUN FACT

Archaeologists discovered a Roman bathhouse in Exeter that was so large, up to 200 soldiers could enjoy a bath at the same time!

Isca is much smaller than Rome, but it is an important city as it controls the whole of the south west of Britain. The only way into the city is through four large gates at the North, East, South and West. My father says the walls will make the city safer for us all.

Our house is built from stone around a courtyard and has many different rooms; some of the floors have mosaics like the houses in Rome. We are very lucky as we have fresh water carried from the springs nearby by a wooden aqueduct into the city. The food here is quite different to Rome. We eat what is grown locally including bread made from wheat and porridge made from oats which are grown in fields outside the city walls. We also eat fish caught from the river which flows just below the city gate. We also have a cockpit which is where you can watch two cockerels fighting. I am hoping father will take me to a cock-fight soon, but he usually says I am too young.

Roman pots like this one were made from clay and would have been used to store food.

How do we know?

Archaeologists didn't think Exeter was very important to the Romans until builders found human remains in front of the Cathedral while they were digging the foundations for a new car park. Archaeologists dug through a Saxon and a Medieval graveyard to discover the remains of a Roman bathhouse under the pavement in front of Exeter Cathedral.

More than 1,000 Roman coins have also been found in the city which tells us that after the soldiers left, Exeter became an important trading town for the Romans. Although the city wall has been repaired many times, parts of the original Roman wall can still be seen all over the city.

The Vikings Attack

The Vikings attack without warning. Like ants, they swarm through the tiny Anglo-Saxon settlement, swinging their axes and hacking down everyone and everything in their path. The air is filled with the smell of smoke as the Vikings set fire to the wooden huts and their straw roofs are soon ablaze. Nine-year-old Arthur and his family escape from their hut, and run for their lives. Their only hope is to find safety in the nearby town of Hlidan.

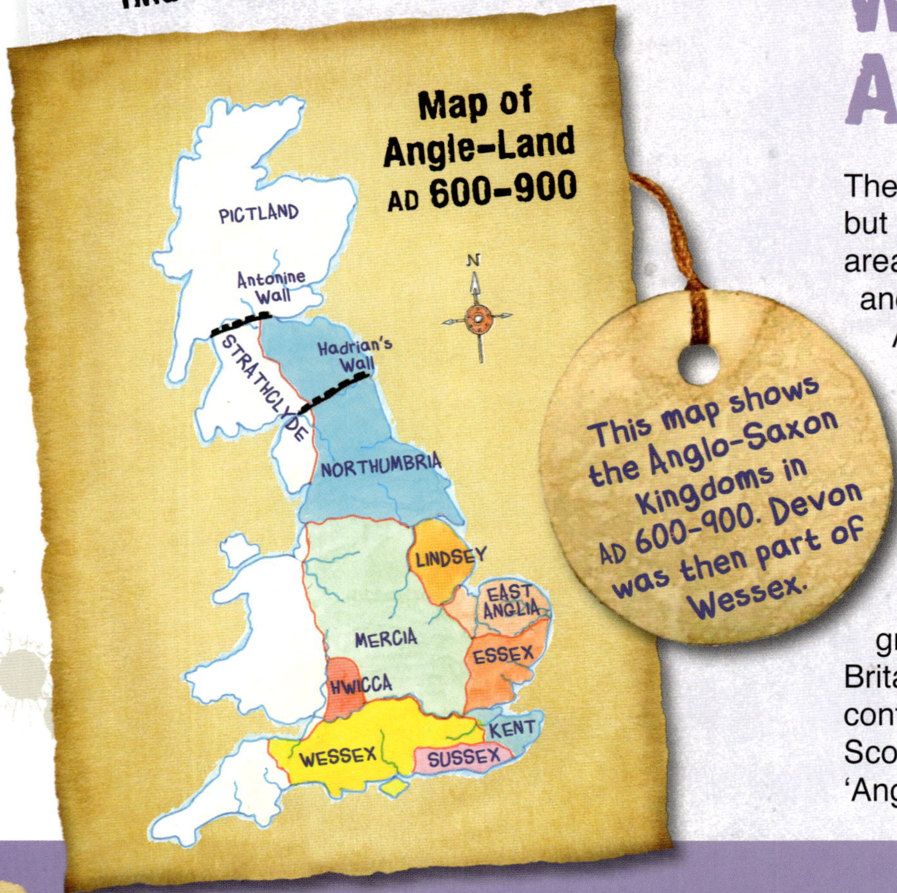

Who were the Anglo-Saxons?

The Anglo-Saxons were not a single tribe, but a mixture of different peoples from the areas of Europe we now know as Denmark and Germany. Among these were the Angles, the Saxons and the Jutes. All of them had fast-growing populations, and were eager to find new land to settle on.

Saxon raiders began attacking the south-east coast of England in about AD 350. After Roman power collapsed in around AD 410, other Anglo-Saxon groups crossed the sea to southern Britain. Within two centuries, they had taken control of all the land up to the borders of Scotland and Wales. It became known as 'Angle-land', or England.

Hlidan

The Anglo-Saxons invaded England in the 5th century. After a great battle in AD 682, they conquered Dyfneint, or Devon as it is called today, and by AD 710 most of Devon was in Anglo-Saxon hands. Most Anglo Saxons were farmers living in small settlements.

Lydford is a small village on the edge of Dartmoor National Park. In Anglo-Saxon times, it was called Hlidan. It was an important place. The town, called a burh, was set up in AD 880 by King Alfred the Great, the Anglo-Saxon king of Wessex, to defend his land against the Vikings and other raiders from Cornwall.

Hlidan was also a centre for making silver coins, or pennies, because it was surrounded by rich silver mines. The people who made the coins were called moneyers.

SPOT THIS!

The stone pillar in Lydford marks the attack in AD 997 where the Vikings 'burned and killed everything that they met'.

Most Saxons lived in huts like this.

FUN FACT

Four original Lydford pennies made by an Anglo-Saxon moneyer still hang in the Castle Inn in Lydford today.

A Holy Place

The Anglo-Saxons brought with them their own Germanic languages. These gradually mixed with the Roman and Celtic speech of the native peoples, and developed into the English language we use today. Many common English words, such as 'hundred', 'ghost', 'night' and 'horse', were originally Anglo-Saxon words.

The Anglo-Saxons also left us another huge legacy. The earliest settlers were pagans. This means they worshipped many different nature gods. But from about AD 600, missionaries from Ireland and mainland Europe converted many people to Christianity. Britain became a Christian country for the first time.

In this imaginary account, a 10-year-old Anglo-Saxon girl called Aethel tells us about her life, living in a settlement near Hlidan in AD 900.

I live in a wooden hut with a straw roof. My father, mother, brother and I all live in one room. We also keep our animals in our house. In the winter, their heat helps warm up the hut.

My father is a farmer. He grows wheat and barley, but also peas, cabbages, carrots and celery. Farming is very hard work and in the winter we have to kill some of the animals as we don't have enough food to feed them and keep them alive. We also raise goats, cows and sheep.

My brother, Lucan, helps my father farm the land. I help Mother with other chores, such as plucking chickens and spinning wool. I also herd the sheep and cattle. I have to be on the lookout all the time because there are wolves that live in the forest nearby.

We are all frightened of the Vikings. When we hear they are coming we run to Hlidan and my father helps defend the village from attack and keep us safe.

SAXON PLACE NAMES

eccles- = church
-ham = homestead
-tun or -ton = village

VIKING PLACE NAMES

kir- = church
-by = homestead or village
-gat = road or way

Do you live somewhere that has a Saxon or Viking name?

FUN FACT

The Saxons built a tall wide bank of stone and earth in Lydford to keep the Vikings out that still exists today.

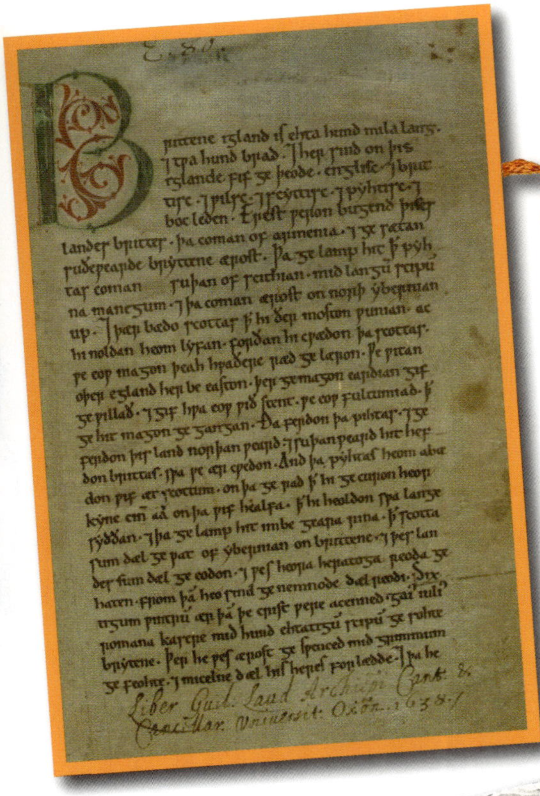

This is a page from the Anglo-Saxon Chronicle which still survives today.

This is a replica of the Lydford Penny. The original coin is over 1,000 years old!

How do we know?

The Viking attack on Lydford is mentioned in the Anglo Saxon Chronicles. The town still has the same layout as it did in Saxon times. It is likely that the original Saxon church of Lydford, which had walls of wood, was constructed during the 8th century. About 1.5 million silver pennies were made from AD 973 to 1066 and they have been found as far away as Russia. There are about 21 Lydford Silver Pennies in the British museum. Lots of Lydford pennies have also been found in Scandinavia and were probably brought back by the Vikings. The Saxons often gave the Vikings the pennies in the hope they wouldn't attack them. We still use English pennies today.

Monasteries grew rich and powerful in Saxon times.

Save Exeter

Edward and his father are standing on the high walls surrounding the city of Exeter. Below them, William the Conqueror and his 400 men wait for the people of Exeter to surrender. People are lining the city walls shouting and jeering at the Norman invaders. Several of William's men are digging tunnels under the walls to try and get into the city. But Exeter will not give in.

Invaders

New invaders landed in Britain in 1066. These were the Normans, from Northern France. Their leader, William, claimed that he had been promised the English throne. The Normans defeated the English army at Hastings, and William was crowned king. He established a strong government, headed by Norman noblemen.

Over the next four centuries, Britain changed from a collection of small kingdoms into just two independent nations. Soon after the Normans took control of all England, they also became overlords of Ireland. In 1282, English armies conquered Wales. Only Scotland remained free from English rule, after defeating them at Bannockburn in 1314.

A sketch of what Exeter Castle may have looked like in Medieval Times.

Under Siege

By 1068, William and his Norman army had reached Devon. Exeter became the first town to resist the Norman invasion. With its high city walls, Exeter was a wealthy city with around 2,500 inhabitants. The mother of King Harold who was killed in the Battle of Hastings lived in Exeter and the people were not willing to swear their loyalty to the new king.

William the Conqueror laid siege to the city for 18 days. He even blinded a person in front of the townsfolk to frighten them into giving up. Finally when William promised not to hurt them, the people of Exeter surrendered. William then built a castle to make sure they behaved in the future.

SPOT THIS!

Can you find the Roman Gatehouse that survives today? It had very small windows.

How do we know?

Exeter Castle, built by William the Conqueror, still exists today. It was called Rougemont Castle which is French for 'red hill' as it was built on volcanic rock which is reddish in colour. The main part of the castle was the gatehouse. Its walls were six feet thick and it was two storeys high.

We know about William's siege on Exeter from Orderic Vitalis. He was a monk who lived just after the time of William the Conqueror. In his book, *The Ecclesiastical History*, he wrote about William the Conqueror's siege of Exeter in 1068, using interviews and documents from the time. He described Exeter as 'a wealthy and ancient city, strongly fortified'.

Ship Ahoy!

John, a ship's cabin boy, is sitting on Plymouth harbour watching cargo being loaded off the giant ships. All around him, the port is filled with the cry of seagulls, the sound of people shouting and ships being built or repaired. The air is filled with the smell of spices brought back from the New World such as cinnamon, cloves and ginger. The galleons with their huge masts connected by a spider's web of ropes and rigging lie in the harbour waiting to set sail to lands that have not yet even been discovered.

Henry VIII made himself head of the church in England.

The Tudors

In 1485, the nobles of Lancaster won the Battle of Bosworth, which ended the Wars of the Roses. This brought a new family to the throne of England – the Tudors. They ruled for more than a century, until 1603, during which huge changes took place in Britain.

The Tudor monarchs were strong and ruthless rulers. Henry VII made the country wealthy and peaceful again after the long civil war. Henry VIII broke England's links with the Roman Catholic Church, and opened the way for the Reformation. And Elizabeth I was a tough and inspiring leader, who survived plots against her life, and threats of invasion from France and Spain.

Francis Drake

Plymouth was an important port during the times of the Tudors. During Queen Elizabeth I's reign, Francis Drake lived in Plymouth and even became mayor. He was an explorer of the New World (Africa, the Americas and West Indies). In 1581 he was awarded a knighthood. Although popular in England he became unpopular with the Spanish who saw him as a pirate as he stole from their treasure ships, making a fortune for the queen and country.

In 1588, the Spanish launched an attack. A huge fleet of ships, known as the Spanish Armada, set sail for Plymouth. Drake fought the Spanish and after a month at sea, defeated the Armada.

SPOT THIS!

Can you find the statue on Plymouth Hoe of Sir Francis Drake?

FUN FACT

Francis Drake was the son of a farmer. He was born in nearby Tavistock and was the eldest of 12 boys.

Peace, Poetry and Plague

The Tudor Age was a dazzling time for Britain. There was a long period of peace at home, while many other parts of Europe were torn by religious wars. This helped the country to become richer. The population grew, and so did farming and other industries. British seamen opened up new trading routes and founded colonies overseas.

The century also produced some of Britain's greatest writers, artists and composers. Greatest of them all was William Shakespeare, whose plays are still performed all over the world. Francis Bacon was one of the founders of modern science.

While the arts and trade prospered, living conditions got worse. With a fast growing population and a lack of hygiene and sanitation the Plague spread killing nearly a third of England's population.

Plymouth harbour is bustling with trade but while some people are getting wealthy others are struggling to survive. This imaginary account is told by a young boy who isn't lucky enough to go to school. He helps in his mother's bakery.

I sell cakes to the sailors that come in on the ships. Sometimes they give me something they have brought back from the New World. One sailor gave me something called a tomato. It was round and red and very juicy. I was also given a potato, but it didn't taste of much.

Every day ships sail in and out of the harbour. The harbour is surrounded by large houses owned by wealthy merchants. They are rich because of all the different food they bring back from the New World, especially sugar which tastes very sweet, but costs a lot of money.

There is not much room in the city so the houses are built upwards, each one having several floors, one above the other. It makes the narrow streets very dark as it blocks the light. There is also a foul smell. The streets aren't safe, so I have to be very careful as there are many people who would steal from my cakes and money.

FUN FACT

Most people lived in houses with thatch roofs. Rodents lived in the thatch and they, and their waste, would fall onto the floors below!

The Merchant's House is Plymouth's best surviving Tudor home.

This is an example of an apothecary in Tudor times. Some apothecaries were known to accept special requests for poison!

How do we know?

We know Sir Francis Drake existed through pictures and documents from the time. There is a portrait of Sir Francis Drake hanging in his former home, Buckland Abbey in Devon that was painted when he was still alive. Richard Hakluyt who was a writer and traveller living during the time of Francis Drake mentions how Drake fought in the Spanish Armada in one of his books. He also wrote about all the different things the English explorers brought back from the New World.

We only need to walk around the Barbican in Plymouth to see many of the buildings still standing from Tudor times. There are over 100!

Tudor kings and queens toured the country, staying at inns and manor houses.

Siege!

Billy watches the Roundheads from the castle walls. They are firing huge cannon balls at the castle as they try to force their way in. It is only a matter of time before they break through. The smell of gunpowder hangs in the air. The sound of muskets and cannons exploding echoes all around. The noise is deafening. Men are shouting and screaming. Others lie injured or dying on the ground. It is a horrible sight.

The Stuarts

The last Tudor monarch, Elizabeth I, died in 1603. She had no children so her cousin James became the new English ruler. He was already King of Scotland, and became James I of England as well. The two countries were united for the first time, though they kept their own laws and parliaments.

James was the first Stuart monarch. He believed kings had been given their right to rule by God and had absolute power. This made him unpopular. He was also threatened by Catholic extremists, who wanted England to be a Catholic country again. In 1605, a group of them tried to kill James in Parliament with explosives. The 'Gunpowder Plot' was discovered just in time.

Pilgrim Fathers

In 1620, a group of people called the Pilgrim Fathers felt they were treated badly because they had different religious beliefs to most people so they decided to go to America. They sailed from Plymouth in a ship called the *Mayflower* in search of a new life. It took 66 days to cross the Atlantic. They were the first people from Europe to settle in North America. They founded one of the country's first towns which they called Plymouth.

The rock that the Pilgrim Fathers first stepped on when they arrived in North America is called Plymouth Rock and can be seen today. When the townspeople of New Plymouth tried to move it, they dropped it and it broke in two.

Civil War

In 1625 James's son, Charles I, became King. He was very unpopular and tried to rule without consulting Parliament. This led to the English Civil War in 1642, fought between supporters of the King and supporters of Parliament. Many people died and there was terrible bloodshed on both sides.

In 1646, there was a battle in Torrington, a town in North Devon. The town supported the King, but after a massive battle in the streets involving 15,000 men, the Parliamentarians led by Sir Thomas Fairfax took the town from the royalists. It was the end of royal resistance in the West Country. In 1649 Charles I was beheaded.

England was now a republic, with no monarch. It was ruled first by Parliament, and then by their leader, Oliver Cromwell. The republic did not last long and, in 1660, the Stuarts returned to the throne. In 1707, England and Scotland officially joined to become the United Kingdom of Great Britain.

FUN FACT

Around 200 royalist prisoners held in Torrington's church were accidentally blown up as the church was used to store 80 barrels of gun powder.

How do we know?

When Torrington's church was destroyed in the explosion, it was rebuilt in 1651 and is today the Parish Church of St Michael and All Angels. Although there have been some changes, the large cobbled 'mound' outside the church door, where the remains of the prisoners' bodies are said to be buried, still remains today.

The anniversary of the battle is remembered every February with a fantastic torch-lit procession when the town turns out in 17th century costume and re-enacts the proclamation of the victorious Sir Thomas Fairfax. 'Torrington 1646' is a great museum all about life during the Stuart Times with lots of fun things to see and do.

Progress and Travel

Elizabeth is too excited to sit still. She is on the train with her parents waiting to arrive at Ilfracombe where her aunt and cousin Mary are waiting to meet them. Mary has told her all about Ilfracombe in her letters. She has made plans for this seaside holiday. They will stroll along the sea front and eat ice cream. They will enjoy a ride in a horse and carriage and go on the merry-go round. Elizabeth is most excited about having a paddle in the sea.

Industrial Britain

By the 18th century manufacturing, mining and farming in Britain were being transformed by the development of steam power and the invention of new machines.The 19th century saw the peak of the Industrial Revolution in Britain. Many people left Devon and flocked to the new manufacturing towns in search of work. Hours were long and wages low, so young children often worked as well as their parents. Living conditions were very cramped with many families sharing one room, with little clean water or sanitation. Medicine was basic and disease spread quickly killing many. Epidemics were common in the cities as well as the country, but it seemed no-one knew how to stop them. Then, in 1829, William Budd, a country doctor from Devon, discovered that diseases could be caught from drinking water that contained sewage and slowly things began to improve. New laws were introduced improving drinking water. New laws also reduced the number of hours women and children could work. Inspectors were appointed to check the safety standards of factories and mines.

The Seaside

During the 19th century, the railway was invented, making it easier for Victorians to travel and visit different parts of the country. For the first time people took holidays. The Victorians liked to visit Devon because of its beautiful beaches and clean air. They thought bathing or swimming was very good for your health. Because of this, towns such as Torquay and Paignton in South Devon and Lynmouth and Ilfracombe in North Devon became very popular with the Victorians.

Ilfracombe used to be a small fishing village on the North Devon coast. Then in 1874, a railway was opened from Barnstaple to Ilfracombe allowing thousands of people to visit it for the first time. People also arrived by paddle steamer from Bristol and Cardiff.

SPOT THIS!

The Ilfracombe tunnels hand-carved out of the rock. They allowed Victorian bathers to reach the beach.

This photograph shows a Victorian school outing to the beach.

The Victorians

By late Georgian times, the British royal family had become very unpopular. People thought their rulers were weak and corrupt. Then in 1837, Victoria became queen of Britain, aged only 18 years old. She reigned for over 60 years until 1901, and restored respect for the monarchy.

During the Victorian Age, the British Empire grew to its greatest size. It covered nearly a quarter of the globe, and included many millions of people. The Empire gave Britain vast supplies of valuable raw materials. It was also a huge market for selling goods manufactured at home. Troops were stationed in most parts of the Empire, giving Britain a lot of power in the world.

... 1871 FIRST MONDAY BANK HOLIDAYS... 1874 TRAINS COME TO BARNSTAPLE...

In this imaginary account, Elizabeth writes to her Grandmama and tells her all about her holiday in Ilfracombe.

Dear Grandmama,

I am having such fun on my holiday with cousin Mary in Ilfracombe. We arrived by train which was very exciting. It travels much faster than a horse and carriage.

I have already had a donkey ride along the beach. Yesterday afternoon I watched the Punch and Judy show. Punch and Judy are puppets. Punch speaks in a very strange way and is very naughty, but it is very funny.

Today we are going to listen to the band playing in the bandstand on the sea front. There is also an arcade with all sorts of machines with pretty lights and music. One machine can even tell your fortune for a penny. I am hoping Mother will let me go.

The town is very pretty with sandy beaches and tall cliffs. You have to walk through a special tunnel to get to the bathing area.

Mother and Father love it here. They say it is much healthier than London. The air is definitely cleaner. I have been bathing every day.

Yours
Elizabeth

Before mixed bathing was introduced in 1905, the women wore bathing costumes down to their knees and the men bathed naked!

The Bath House was built in 1836. On the right is the Tunnels Beaches entrance.

FUN FACT
Every June, the people of Ilfracombe dress up in Victorian clothing to celebrate the town's Victorian history.

This is a Victorian camera. The leather bellows were moved in or out to change the focus.

How do we know?

The hand-carved tunnels in Ilfracombe still exist today, along with photographs of Victorians bathing in the waters. Photography had just been invented in Victorian times, with the first photographs being taken in the 1830s.

There are many stories from visitors and people living in Ilfracombe at the time about what life was like during Victorian times. The Ilfracombe Museum is a treasure trove of fascinating objects and pictures from the time. Information boards have been put up all over the town, showing photographs of holidaymakers of old. There was also a superb tidal sea water swimming pool which children still swim in today. Many of the houses on the hills surrounding the bay were built during Victorian times.

Wartime

Everywhere buildings are on fire. The sky is bright orange from the flames and the heat is almost unbearable. Robbie flees his house with his sister and gran, running to take cover in the bomb shelter at the bottom of the garden. The hum of hundreds of enemy planes can be heard overhead, followed by the whistle of bombs dropping on the city. Every now and then there is another explosion as a bomb hits its target. The noise is deafening.

World Wars

When Queen Victoria died in 1901, Britain was one of the world's most powerful nations, with a massive empire and strong armed forces. But soon the British were plunged into long and costly world wars. In World War One (1914-1918), over a million men were killed.

World War Two (1939-1945) killed a vast number of civilians as well as soldiers. Enemy bombs destroyed large areas of major towns.The cost of the fighting left Britain with huge debts. The British Empire began to shrink, as many countries demanded their freedom.

The Blitz

Devon's position meant it was heavily exposed to enemy attack by air and sea. Okehampton had an RAF base which assisted the army and patrolled the coastlines. Torquay was one seaside resort requisitioned by the RAF. Many American troops were stationed in Torquay in 1944.

Plymouth was a main target because of its dockyards at nearby Devonport. For hundreds of years ships were built there for the navy and were used to help defend the country.

During World War Two, there were 59 bombing raids on the city in what became known as the 'blitz'. Plymouth was one of the worst-bombed cities in the country. The city centre was almost completely destroyed and 1,174 civilians were killed. Nearly 4,000 homes were destroyed and more than 8,000 were seriously damaged.

Hard Times

Britain took a long time to recover from the effects of World War Two. But by the 1960s the economy had grown strong again. In 1973, Britain joined the Common Market (now called the European Union), an organisation which aimed to bring the countries of Europe closer together. In 1994 the Channel Tunnel was completed, linking Britain with mainland Europe.

There were also big changes in the way the British nations ruled themselves. In 1998, an agreement between the governments of Northern Ireland and the Irish Republic brought peace after 30 years of unrest and violence. In 1999, the people of Scotland and Wales voted to have their own parliaments and make many of their own laws.

SPOT THIS!

Charles Church, in Plymouth, was nearly destroyed during the bombing in 1941. It has been preserved in memory of those who were killed.

War-time gas masks looked like this and protected against gas attacks.

FUN FACT

Plymouth has more post-war listed buildings than anywhere in England outside London.

Robbie lives in Plymouth. His mum is an air raid warden and his dad is away with the Navy. He hasn't seen his dad in two years. In this imaginary account, he talks about life in Plymouth during the war.

Plymouth has been bombed for six nights in a row. Buildings everywhere are on fire. My Nan, sister and I are in our shelter at the bottom of the garden. We are praying that we won't be hit by a bomb. It is very scary as I can hear bombs exploding all around us.

Mum has left the shelter and gone to do her job. I think she's very brave. When there is threat of attack she has to go and work with the other air raid wardens. She carries a bucket of sand and her job is to put out the fires caused by the thousands of small bombs dropped by the Germans. We all miss Dad. He's been away fighting in this awful war for over two years. We haven't heard from him in a couple of weeks. I hope he's ok.

Mum says the German bombers are trying to destroy the warships in the dockyards at Devonport, but most of the bombs seem to be hitting people's houses, shops and even the cinemas. My school has already been destroyed. I don't think there is much left of Plymouth.

Mum says me and Annie are to go to live with our aunty until the war is over. Aunty has a farm on Dartmoor so it may be fun. A lot of my friends have already left the city.

Government Air Raid Warning in 1939:

When you hear the warning take cover at once. Remember that most of the injuries in an air raid are caused not by direct hits by bombs but by flying fragments of debris or by bits of shells.

Sirens sounded to warn people that they were under attack by enemy planes. They had to take cover in air raid shelters.

Here is a week's worth of food rations for one adult.

one egg
meat costing 6p
100g bacon and ham
50g cheese
180 ml milk
225g sugar
50g jam
50g tea
88g of sweets or chocolate

Many people kept their ration books after the war, giving us plenty of evidence of how rationing worked.

How do we know?

Some fighter and bomber pilots and Navy officers from World War Two are still alive today. Their stories are often posted on the internet and there are many programmes on television that talk of their experiences.

There are also many people who were children during the Blitz who are still alive today and can remember what it was like during World War Two. Many photographs and diaries written by children at the time have survived.

Groups of people re-enact scenes from World War Two. This helps to bring the period to life. There are also war memorials, dedicated to all those who died during the war.

Today and Tomorrow

Today Devon is a busy, thriving county. Many people still work as farmers just as they did 2,000 years ago. Every year, thousands of visitors come to Devon to visit its ancient sites and medieval castles, such as Powderham Castle near Exeter or Okehampton Castle, which is mentioned in the Doomsday book and is said to be haunted.

The biggest show of the year is the Devon County Show. Farmers from all over the country bring their prize bulls, cows and sheep to compete against each other for the top prize.

You can feel proud to be from Devon!

Devon is also very lucky to have not one, but two national parks called Exmoor and Dartmoor which are famous for having their own ponies.

Devon is also well known for its amazing beaches. Both North Devon and South Devon have miles and miles of sandy beaches, such as Saunton Sands in the North and Dawlish Warren in the South.

...2010 POPULATION OF DEVON AROUND 1.4 MILLION...

FUN FACT

Some dinosaur fossils have been found on the Jurassic Coast. An enormous Crocodile head was found in 2009 and is 130 million years old!

South East Devon is also known as the Jurassic Coast. The rocks that line the coast are 180 million years old. Some incredible dinosaur fossils have been found here.

The National Marine Aquarium in Plymouth is the largest aquarium in the country.

Devon is a very old county and many of its festivals and fairs date back hundreds of years. Chulmleigh fair in North Devon has taken place every year since 1253. The Money Scramble is one of the most ancient customs and still enjoyed today!

How will they know?

How will future generations know what Devon was like for us, now? The internet is a great way of recording the present. Photos, blogs and stories from tourists can all spread the word about our wonderful county. Hundreds of years from now someone may be looking at your picture or reading your blog. You're making history!

Glossary

AD – a short way of writing the Latin words anno Domini, which mean 'in the year of our Lord', i.e. after the birth of Christ.

Anglo Saxon Chronicle – a collection of records that tell the history of the Anglo Saxon period.

Apothecary – a person who prepared and sold medicines and drugs.

Aqueduct – a channel built to carry water.

Archaeologist – a person who studies the past by looking at the remains left by people in the past.

Basilica – a large Roman building similar to a town hall.

BC – a short way of writing 'before the birth of Christ'.

Blitz – when the Germans bombed towns during World War Two, it was called 'the Blitz'.

British Empire – the territories around the world colonised by Britain from the 17th century. Most are now independent countries.

Catholic – a member of the Christian religion that considers the Pope to be the head of its church.

Christian – a religion based on the life and teachings of Jesus of Nazareth.

Domesday Book – William the Conqueror sent his men all over England to check how much land and wealth was in the kingdom, and who owned it. The results of this survey were written in a book called the Domesday Book, which survives to this day.

Harbour – a sheltered port where ships can load and unload cargo.

Industrial Revolution – a period from the 18th to the 19th century where big changes in agriculture, manufacturing, mining, and transport occurred, beginning with the invention of steam-powered machines.

Merchant – a person who buys and sells goods in order to make a living.

Monastery – a place where monks live and worship.

Monk – a male member of a religious community that has rules of poverty, chastity and obedience.

Mosaic – a design made up of small pieces of glass or stone.

Musket – a long-barrelled gun, loaded from the front, used from the 16th to the 18th centuries.

New World – the name for North and South America during the 15th century.

Pagan – someone who believes in more than one god.

Plague (Black Death) – a serious disease that is carried by rats and can be transferred to humans by fleas.

Protestant – a member of the Christian religion that considers the king or queen to be the head of its church.

Puritan – Protestants who wanted a simpler form of the Church of England.

Roundhead – anyone who fought on the side of Parliament against Charles I in the English Civil War.

Siege – when people try to capture a place by surrounding or blockading it.

Index

Acknowledgements

The publishers would like to thank the following people and organizations for their permission to reproduce material on the following pages:

p4: Courtesy of Exeter Archaeology; p6: riekephotos/Shutterstock; p7: Fishbourne Museum, Chichester; p9: Copyright D W Palmer www.lydford.co.uk; p11: Lindisfarne gospe public domain/Wiki, Copyright D W Palmer www.lydford.co.uk; p12: www.exetercastle.co.uk; p15: Shutterstock; p21: Tunnels Beaches, Ilfracombe, Devon www.tunnelsbeaches.co.uk; p22: Tunnels Beaches, Ilfracombe, Devon www.tunnelsbeaches.co.uk; p23: Swindon Museum; p25: York Museums Trust; p27: Shutterstock; p28: (t) Chulmleigh Old Fair Archive www.chulmleigh.org, (c) Visit Devon, (b) Tunnels Beaches, Ilfracombe, Devon www.tunnelsbeaches.co.uk; p29: (t) Visit Devon, (b) Chulmleigh Old Fair Archive www.chulmleigh.org

All other images copyright of Hometown World

Every effort has been made to trace and acknowledge the ownership of copyright. If any rights have been omitted, the publishers offer to rectify this in any future editions.

Written by Tina Orr Munro
Designed by Sarah Allen and Siân Williams
Edited by Carly Corlett
Local history consultant: Anne Morgan

Illustrated by Kate Davies, Dynamo Ltd, Virginia Gray,
Peter Kent, Kevin Kimber, John MacGregor, Leighton Noyes and Tim Sutcliffe
Additional photographs by Alex Long

First published by HOMETOWN WORLD in 2012
Hometown World Ltd
7 Northumberland Buildings
Bath BA1 2JB

www.hometownworld.co.uk

ISBN 978-1-84993-231-8

Printed in China

CELT
500 BC
ROMAN
AD 43–410
ANGLO-SAXON
AD 450–1066
VIKING
AD 865–1066
MEDIEVAL TIMES
1066–1485